THE POETRY PROCESSOR

BOOK 2

Paul Higgins

SIMON & SCHUSTER
EDUCATION

CONTENTS

TO THE STUDENT

The Poetry Processor gives you the chance to explore poetry, to write poems yourself, and to read and enjoy poems written by other people.

Poetry is powerful.
- Poetry can help you to use words more skilfully and imaginatively
- Poetry can help you to find pleasure in words
  - in their music, through rhythm, rhyme and sound
  - in their meanings, through wordplay and riddles
  - in their pattern, through the way they join together to make a whole poem
- Poetry can be a way of speaking about things that matter to you
- Poetry can make you more aware of the world around you
- Poetry can help you to discover things about yourself and other people
- Poetry can challenge, shock, provoke and surprise.

Poetry is everywhere, from playground chants and nursery rhymes to songs and adverts.

This book shows you some of the many different types of poetry that you can find, and that you can write anytime, anywhere.

Paul Higgins

1 RHYMING CHAT
What about that?

When rhyme is mentioned we usually think of poetry, but in the following sketch from the series *The Two Ronnies*, rhyme is part of the conversation. There are two characters in the sketch. In pairs, read it aloud, taking a part each.

THE CASE OF MRS MACE   Gerald Wiley

(The scene is a police station – Ronnie Barker, a plain-clothes North Country detective, sits at a desk. Ronnie Corbett enters.)

Ronnie Corbett: Good day, Inspector Jay.
Ronnie Barker: Morning, Dorning. Any news of the Girder Murder?
C: Yessir. He's been shot at Oxshott. Bagshot got him with a slingshot full of buckshot.
B: He's a good shot, Bagshot. Well, you must be pleased that situation's eased.
C: The relief is beyond belief, chief. My mind is once more a blank. And I've only you to thank.
B: All right. Never mind the fawning, Dorning. I'm glad to hear your head's clear: it means there's more space for the Mrs Mace case to take its place.

C: The Mrs Mace case? Have they traced the face? (*Points to photofit blow-up on the wall.*)

B: No – and the night-dress is still missing.

C: Any prospects of any suspects?

B: Yes – two. Two of them are actors who lodge with Grace – Mrs Mace, at her place in the Chase. Leo Mighty, the leading man, known for his portrayals of charmers, farmers, and men in pyjamas. And the other one is Roger Mainger, the stage manager, who once played a mad stranger in a film starring Stewart Grainger called 'Deadly Danger'.

C: May I add another to your list? If I'm not being too bumptious or presumptious?

B: Who?

C: Sergeant Bodger!

B: What? That replacement constable from Dunstable? You must be crazy.

C: It's just a theory, dearie. May I sit down?

B: Please – make yourself comfry, Humphrey.

C: (*Sitting down*) It's just that Bodger has got a face like a fit: which fits the face on the photofit in the first place, and he's often to be found at her place, in the Chase, filling his face with fish.

B: Fish?

C: Fried by Grace – Mrs Mace. Mostly Dace – or Plaice.

B: But what about Leo Mighty? He's there nightly – isn't it slightly more likely? She obviously looks flighty in her nighty – he's the sort of toff that might try to pull it off.

C: Possibly – but here's something you don't know.

B: I don't.

C: No. I've spoken with Roger.

B: Roger?

C: The lodger.

B: Oh – Roger Mainger, who played the stranger with Grainger.

C: He says he saw Leo take the night-gown. He was staring through the keyhole in Mrs Mace's bedroom door.

B: He dared to stare through there? Would he swear he saw Leo Mighty take the nighty?

C: He'll do plenty of swearing. No wonder he was staring – it was the one she was wearing!

B: What? Surely not!

C: He stood on the bed, and pulled it over her head. She went red, and he fled. He locked himself in the shed, and wished he were dead. She was going to phone her cousin Ted, but felt dizzy in the head, so she lay on the bed instead, and went red.

B: So you said. I've seen where Mrs Mace sleeps. It's an attic! So the story about pulling the garment over her head is false. He would have to pull the night-gown right down! There's no headroom in her bedroom!

C: So Roger's lying! Then he must be the culprit! Game, set and match, chief! And so ends the disgraceful Grace Mace case.

B: (*Picks up the phone*) I'll just tell the Chief Constable – what a relief, constable. (*Into phone*) Hello sir – we've solved the Mace case. I'm happy to tell you that Leo is innocent, and so is Sergeant Bodger. Yes sir: in other words – 'twas not Leo Mighty who lifted the nighty, 'twas Roger the Lodger, the soft-footed dodger, and not Sergeant Bodger, thank God!

Writing a rhyming sketch is a challenge and gives an opportunity for you to improve your skill in making rhymes.

Here is a short rhyming conversation written by two second year girls.

OUT AND ABOUT, STOPPING AND SHOPPING
Rebecca Teasdale and Adele Humphrey

Mrs Grey: Hello Mr. Snow.

Mr. Snow: Good day, Mrs Grey. Pray, what can I do for you?

G: Have you any socks in your stocks?

S: Well, yesterday we had lots of socks in our stocks, but they have gone. We have none. But wait! I see one pair, there on the stair.

G: They seem to be cream. That won't do. I wanted blue.

S: I'm afraid, dear, that it's really clear, I fear, that we haven't got another sock in stock.

G: Oh no, is that so, Mr. Snow? Well, I really must go. Never mind the socks. Mr. Fox has got lots in a box in his shop. Oh, I must go. Cheerio, Mr. Snow!

(*She leaves the shop.*)

G: (*Thinking aloud*) Oh, I'll get the socks from Mr. Fox in a couple of tocks, but right now I'll hop into the butcher's shop. (*Enters shop.*) Hello Mr. Quince. Have you got any mince?

Mr. Quince: No, Mrs Snow, I've only the pork that arrived from York, or there's the ham from Birmingham, or maybe you'd like some mutton from Sutton – Coldfield that is.

G: Well I'd rather have mince, Mr. Quince, but since you have none I'll be gone. Goodbye, Mr. Quince! I'll come back for the mince.

Q: Good day, Mrs Grey. Have a nice day!

MORE THINGS TO DO

1. In pairs, record one of the two sketches above onto tape, or practise reading it aloud for a performance to the rest of the class.
2. Either on your own, or in pairs, write your own rhyming conversation between two people, e.g.

   A: Hello mate!
   B: You're late. You said you'd be at the gate by eight.
   A: Don't get in a state. You didn't have to wait.
   B: Where are we going, now it's snowing?
   A: Not down the park. It's too dark . . . etc.

Look again at how a conversation written in play form is set out. You do not need to use speech marks, but go on to a new line every time there is a new speaker and put a colon after the name of the speaker.

Name Colon Speech

Jill: Hello mate!
Jane: You're late . . .

When you have completed your rhyming sketch, you could read it aloud to the rest of the class, record it onto tape, or even act it out.

2 Cleri who? CLERIHEW!

A clerihew is the strange name for a particular type of short, humorous, rhyming poem. The poems below are all clerihews. In pairs, read them aloud and try to discover how a clerihew works.

Edward the Confessor
Slept under the dresser.
When that began to pall,
He slept in the hall.

Edmund Clerihew Bentley

Sir Christopher Wren
Said, 'I am going to dine with some men.
If anybody calls
Say I am designing St. Paul's.'

Edmund Clerihew Bentley

Mr Bram Stoker
Was a bit of a joker;
Either that or he
Had bats in his belfry.

Charles Connell

Coleridge, Samuel Taylor
Wrote about an old sailor.
As a Coleridge fan,
I prefer 'Kubla Khan'.

Charles Connell

The Art of Biography
Is different from Geography.
Geography is about Maps
Biography is about Chaps.

Edmund Clerihew Bentley

Jane Austen
Got lost in
Stoke-on-Trent.
Moral: She shouldn't have went.

Roger McGough

Clerihews follow clear rules. Divide into pairs or small groups. Look carefully at the examples and try to work out the rules for a clerihew. The following questions will help you.

a What do all the first lines have in common?
b How many lines are there in each clerihew?
c Do the lines rhyme? If so, what is the rhyme scheme?
d Do the lines have a clear rhythm with a set number of heavy beats?

It's all in the name

The special feature of clerihews is that they are based on the name of a person or a subject and that this name is always the first line of the poem. Clerihews are made up of two rhyming couplets (See Book One, Unit 6). The rhythm is not strictly laid down. The lines can be of different lengths, with different numbers of stresses in them. Clerihews take their name from the man who invented them, Sir Edmund CLERIHEW Bentley.

Here are some clerihews by pupils:

Mike Tyson
Is built like a bison.
When he gives them a clout,
His opponents are down and out.

Simon Montgomery

Dame Edna Everage
Drank gin as her beverage.
She passed out in Newquay
With the words, 'I'm feeling spooky.'

Jane Chapman

Diego Maradona
Showed he had no honour.
Versus England he decided to cheat
But now he is back to using his feet.

Marc Sinfield

Terry Wogan
Has got his own slogan.
These days he says, 'Peace my children!' more and more
No wonder he is such a bore.

Tracy Jenkins

Andy Crane,
Has he got a brain?
There must be something the matter
Because, like the mad hatter, all he does is natter and chatter.

Paul Higgins

MORE THINGS TO DO

1 Try writing some clerihews yourself:

- ♦ Make a list of names of people or subjects which you would like to use; for example, pop stars, sports personalities, politicians, school subjects etc. If you can't think of any suitable names, you can look for some in magazines.
- ♦ Think of a rhyme for your name. If you can't find a rhyme for the surname, then you can swap the two parts of the name around. If you do this, there needs to be a pause between the surname and the first name, shown by a comma. So, for example, Steve Davis swapped round would be

Davis, Steve.

- ♦ Complete the poem by adding another rhyming couplet which rounds off your poem.

When you have written some clerihews, read them aloud in small groups.

2 Book 1 suggested that you could keep a special exercise book for your own anthology. Copy out in your anthology any clerihews that you particularly like. You might find some in published poetry anthologies in the library, or you could choose one or two written by other pupils in your class.

REMEMBER
Clerihews
Aren't too difficult to use.
Choose a name and a rhyme
And don't worry about rhythm and time.

---

3 HAIKU

Haiku is a Japanese form of poetry. It has only three short lines. Read the haiku below, silently.

> Alone I cling to
>   The freezing mountain and see
>   White cloud below me.

Ian Serraillier

Still in silence, read the poem once or twice more. Take your time. Give each word close attention. What ideas and feelings come into your mind?

Now discuss your thoughts about the poem with a partner. Then, in your pairs, discuss the following questions:

a Where does the poet say he is?
b What do the words 'alone', 'cling' and 'freezing' suggest about what he is experiencing and how he is feeling?
c What is striking about the last line?

If you discuss this poem carefully you will find that in just three short lines the writer is saying a great deal. This can be done because in a haiku you do not explain what you think. You show your thoughts by choosing bare and simple details and images which can be read in an instant. A haiku is a snapshot in words.

A good way to appreciate a haiku is to read the poem in silence, not once, but a few times, letting the meanings slowly unfold in your mind. In this way, read the two haiku below. Then, in pairs, discuss your thoughts and feelings about them. When you have done that, discuss the questions which follow each poem.

THE WILD GEESE LEAVE

> Wild geese! I know
>   that they did eat the barley;
>   yet when they go . . .

Yasui (Translated by Harold G. Hobson)

a What is the bad thing about the geese?
b What could, 'Yet when they go . . .' mean?
c What feelings could the writer have towards the geese?

BEAUTY

The usually hateful crow:
  he, too – this morning,
    on the snow!

Matsuo Basho (translated by Harold G. Hobson)

a How does the writer usually feel towards the crow?
b What could be striking about the way the crow looks against the snow?
c Why do you think the writer called the poem 'Beauty'?

Haiku and Syllables

If you say words aloud you can hear each separate part which is sounded. Take the word 'divided'. This has three separately-sounded parts:

   1 2 3
   di-vi-ded.

Each separately-sounded part is a 'syllable'. So the word 'divided' has three syllables.

'Teacher' has two syllables: teach-er
'Children' has two syllables: chil-dren
Words like 'dog' and 'cat' have only one syllable.

In the three short lines of a haiku, there are usually only 17 syllables in all. The first and third lines should have 5 syllables each and the second line should have 7. This syllable rule is only a guideline. You can change the pattern slightly if you need to. For instance, both of the poems below are effective haiku, but only one follows the 5,7,5 rule exactly.

A bitter morning:
  sparrows sitting together
    without any necks.

J. W. Hackett

Fallen flower I see
  returning to its branch –
    Ah! A butterfly.

A. Moritake

Which haiku does not quite fit the 5,7,5 pattern?

Counting the syllables is only a way of encouraging you to choose every word carefully.

13

In silence, read the following haiku poems written by people of your own age.

Mushroom in the sky
  eighty-thousand people die
    without knowing why.

Samantha Hicks

The child who is deaf
  lies listening to the sounds
    within his body.

Alan Schofield

Deer on the mountain
  scraping up the coarse grasses.
    Winter life is hard.

Ann Taylor

The calm countryside
  is disturbed by this buzzing.
    Not bees, but machines!

Sarah Billings

The waves of the sea
  destroying, fighting, angry
    crashing at the rocks.

Claire Curtis

A class in silence
  works through an English lesson
    heads bent over books.

Katy Woodbridge

FOX HUNT

All done without thought.
> Dogs taste blood. A fox is caught.
> They call it sport.

Vivien Markovic

FERRY DISASTER

A duty ignored.
> Screams and cries as the sea roars
> and seals a hundred graves.

Vivien Markovic

Divide into pairs or groups and pick one or two of the poems to discuss. If the poem has a title, discuss how it adds to the meaning of the poem.

MORE THINGS TO DO

1 You should always be thoughtful about the words you use when you are writing poetry, but in a haiku this is especially important. Try writing some haiku poems yourself. Here are some points to bear in mind:

♦ A haiku has only three lines and usually only 17 syllables in all. You do not have to stick exactly to the number of syllables, but you do need three lines.

♦ Do not divide words at the end of a line; e.g. the example below would be wrong even though it follows the haiku pattern:

> The trouble with hai-
> > ku is that you don't have ve-
> > ry many words to . . .

♦ Don't rush to finish a haiku. Take your time.
♦ A thoughtful title will make your meaning clearer.
♦ You can write about anything you like – a memory, a feeling, an experience, an action, a gesture, an idea, a mental picture.

REMEMBER
In a haiku you don't explain what you think. You show your thoughts through simple details and images.

---

2 Find some more haiku to read. Write out any you particularly like in your anthology.

4 SIMILES AND METAPHORS

In the section 'Riddles' similes and metaphors were mentioned (see Book 1, Unit 14), but they are so important that it's a good idea to look at them again in more detail.

When we use a simile we say that one thing is *like* something else. We all use similes in our daily conversation: e.g. He was as quiet as a mouse; She was as busy as a bee; I was shaking like a leaf.

With a metaphor we say one thing *is* another thing. We all use metaphors from time to time: e.g. My feet are blocks of ice; I was burning with rage; That man is a rat.

Similes and metaphors are *images* used to describe things and people. In making images we use our *imagination*.

The problem with the examples of similes and metaphors above is that they are not new. They are *clichés*, or stale and worn-out images. Sometimes clichés are deliberately used in writing, but generally the similes and metaphors used in poetry should be new, original and *imaginative*.

Here is a list of metaphors for the moon which was written by a class. In pairs, read the list aloud. You could do this by taking turns to read a line.

THE MOON IS . . .

The moon is a silver coin on a black blanket.
The moon is a ball of cheese where mice have eaten at it.
The moon is a lighthouse in the sea of night.
The moon is the pale face of a child in fright.
The moon's silver comes to earth and puts some sparkle in the water.
The moon is a gigantic light-bulb lighting up the night sky.
The moon is a boiled potato.
The moon is a golf ball driven through space.

The moon is a floating balloon.
The moon is a football kicked into the sky.
The moon is an apple cut in two.
The moon is a snowball hurtling through a dark winter's night.
The moon is a floodlight shining on the stadium of earth.
The moon is an eye looking down on the sordid world.
The moon is a ship sailing through the night.
The moon is a button, thus 'Button Moon'.
The moon is a question.
The moon is the ghost of a planet.
The moon is my reflection.

♦ Discuss these metaphors, saying which you think are most effective and which do not work so well, and why.
♦ Do you think any of the metaphors in the list are clichés? If you do say which ones and why.

MORE THINGS TO DO

Your imagination is like muscles (simile) because it needs exercise. Try the following exercises as a work-out for your imagination.

Imaginaerobics
There are three ways of playing the game *Imaginaerobics*.

1 Divide into small groups. Each person takes it in turn to think of an object. Everyone in the group writes down one metaphor for the object, within a minute.
2 Within your small group, agree on an object to write about. Write down as many metaphors for it as you can in a set time (say, five minutes).
3 Choose an object (or animal or person). Then pass a sheet of paper round the group or the class, each person adding one metaphor to the list. (The collection of metaphors for the moon was written by a class in this way.) Read your list of metaphors carefully. In your group, discuss which images work best and whether you have used any clichés. Turn your collection of metaphors into a group poem: you can change the order, get rid of stale images and add more details if you like.

Here are some possible subjects:
     fire   rain   a hedgehog   the sun   a teacher
  a vacuum cleaner   the sea   the dark   a snail   television

5 SIMILE POEMS

The following poem is about the poet who wrote it. In it he uses many similes to describe himself. Can you spot any?

THE WRITER OF THIS POEM   Roger McGough

The writer of this poem
Is taller than a tree
As keen as the North Wind
As handsome as can be

As bold as a boxing-glove
As sharp as a nib
As strong as scaffolding
As tricky as a fib

As smooth as lolly-ice
As quick as a lick
As clean as a chemist-shop
As clever as a $\surd$

The writer of this poem
Never ceases to amaze
He's one in a million billion
(or so the poem says!)

A string of similes could be used to describe a different idea, as in the next poem:

USELESS   Paul Higgins

You're as useless
as a bucket with a hole
as a mine without some coal
as a key without a lock
as a tick without a tock

As useless
as a sky without the birds
as a book without the words
as a glove without a hand
as a snapped elastic band

As useless
as a curve without a bend
as a story without an end
as a punctured rubber tyre
as the promise of a liar

As useless
as a record with a scratch
as a cancelled football match
as a fair without the fun
as a rhyme that doesn't work

As useless
as an oil–polluted sea
as a cold cup of tea
as a gift that isn't free
In fact you're almost as useless
as me.

MORE THINGS TO DO

1 As in the first poem above, write a simile poem of your own which describes you. You can use a regular rhythm and rhyme scheme, or just simply write a list of images. Start with the same phrase, 'The writer of this poem is . . .'

As intelligent as a . . .
As courageous as a . . .
As friendly, adventurous, lively, marvellous, brilliant, thrilling, strong, stupendous, beautiful, wonderful, clever, incredible . . .

2 You could write your own 'Useless' poem using a string of different similes, or you could try a different main idea, e.g. 'Lonely' or 'Friendly', 'Sad', 'Happy', 'Shocking', 'Infuriating' etc.

6 JUMBLED RHYMES

Two poems have been cut up into their separate lines and mixed together in any order. Each poem has a regular rhyme and rhythm pattern, and also tells a simple story. The titles in capital letters have also been given as another clue. See if you can sort the lines into the two poems again, in the order which you think works best.

'Crawling is pleasant, but rest is best.'

Searching for a water-hole

Searching for a drink;

Then on again we stumble,

Of flower and leaf – and tiger!

'Oh, earth is good for a butterfly,

To find that Winter had gone away.

To cool our heavy feet.

And we watch the way he went.

We find a spilling river,

Trample on the grasses;

Then stop and breathe the scent

THE TIRED CATERPILLAR

But the sky is best when we learn to fly!'

He felt and fluttered his golden wings:

And into it we sink.

In a hole in the forest, snug and deep.

No need to crawl over sticks and things.

A tired old caterpillar went to sleep

We're swaying through the jungle

All tightly up in his blanket rolled,

He slept through the Winter long and cold,

Dizzy with the heat

And he said, as he softly curled in his nest . . .

ELEPHANTS WALKING

But at last he woke on a warm Spring day

Remember that there are six main clues:

♦ the rhythm (count the number of heavy beats in each line)
♦ the rhymes
♦ the story
♦ the titles
♦ the punctuation
♦ the sense.

When you have completed the exercise, discuss in groups or as a class the various solutions which people came up with. Which ones work best and why? Finally, read the two poems in their original order (you can find them on page 79). How close are they to the versions you produced?

7 LIMERICKS

There was a young farmer from Leeds
Who swallowed a packet of seeds.
In a month, silly ass,
He was covered with grass
And he couldn't sit down for the weeds.

Anon

A limerick is a short, humorous rhyming poem. It has a very clear and familiar rhyme and rhythm pattern. Many of you probably know some limericks. If so, perhaps you could recite one to a partner, or even to the rest of the class. Here are some limericks written by pupils. In pairs or small groups, read them aloud to each other.

There was a young man from Penzance
Who went out one night to a dance.
He did a waltz there
Spinning into the air
And now the man's landed in France.

Paula Card

There was a young fellow called Fred
Who didn't like using his head.
He said when he thought,
It hurt, so he bought
A computer to work with instead.

David Thyer

A young cricket player from Neath
Got a red cricket ball in the teeth.
He spat out a molar
And said to the bowler,
'A little more care if you pleath.'

Andrew Hickey

There was a young boy called McMurray
Who fell deep in love with beef curry.
He said, 'I'll have four!'
And then had still more
And so left the room in a hurry.

Leslee Jolley

There was a young woman from Twickenham
Who bought boots so she could walk quick in 'em.
When out for a walk
She stopped for a talk
And her pet poodle then began lickin' 'em.

Binit Shah

A bionic man from Canthrust
Thought swimming an absolute must,
Till he fell in his pool.
Now he feels such a fool
'Cos his parts you can't reach are just rust.

Rakesh Sharma

In a limerick, the rhymes and rhythm work closely together to give the words that familiar jaunty and humorous effect. The first, second and fifth lines rhyme and the third and fourth lines rhyme. Also, when the rhyme changes, the rhythm changes too. The third and fourth lines have two heavy beats instead of three.

The pattern looks like this:

	STRESSES
There was a young lady from Ryde	(3)
Who ate some green apples and died	(3)
The apples fermented	(2)
Inside the lamented	(2)
And made cider inside her inside.	(3)

This looks complicated, but it isn't really. You can usually tell simply from the sound whether a limerick works or not. Nevertheless it is a good idea to practise the rhyme and rhythm pattern before trying to write your own limericks from scratch.

MORE THINGS TO DO

1 In the following examples the limericks all have the first line and the rhyming words at the end of every line. What you have to do is fill in the lines with something that makes sense and which has the right rhythm. For example,

> A sea serpent saw a big tanker,
> _____ sank her.
> _____ crew
> _____ two,
> _____ anchor.

could be completed, as in the original version, like this:

> A sea serpent saw a big tanker,
> Bit a hole in her side and then sank her.
> It swallowed the crew
> In a minute or two,
> And then picked its teeth with the anchor.

or it could be completed as in this version written by a second year girl:

> A sea serpent saw a big tanker
> And with a swish of her tail she sank her.
> She drowned all the crew
> Including the two
> Who were still hanging on to the anchor.

Louise Potter

You may like to work in pairs. You may also like to turn this activity into a game. You could get into pairs or small groups. Each pair or group is then given one of the unfinished limericks to complete. The first one to complete it in the right rhythm wins.

> A Roman called Julius Caesar,
> _____ sneezer.
> _____ blew.
> _____ through
> _____ geezer.

> There was an old man of Dunoon
> _____ spoon.
> _____ eat
> _____ meat
> _____ soon.

24

There was a young man of
Tralee
_____ knee.
_____ hurt
_____ dirt
_____ three.

A boy who watched all of 'Jaws 2'
_____ blue.
_____ night
_____ fright
_____ do.

There was a young man from
East Fife,
_____ wife.
_____ long
_____ wrong
_____ life.

A man who was mad about honey
_____ money.
_____ life
_____ knife
_____ funny.

2 You can take the idea of incomplete limericks a stage further by writing some incomplete ones of your own for other people to complete. Do this in pairs or small groups. Each person writes the first line of a limerick and the rhyming words for the other four lines. Take it in turns to give your partner, or the rest of the group, your unfinished limerick to complete.

3 Try to write some Consequence Limericks. Get into groups of five. Each person takes a turn to write a line of a group limerick. Don't fold the page over, just add your line to the ones which have gone before. Finally, the person who wrote the first line reads the complete limerick to the rest of the group. (If you have fewer than five in the group, some people will have more than one turn to write a line.) Make a collection of the limericks written by your group and then read them to the rest of the class.

4 Write your own limericks from scratch. You can use any idea and choose any topic you wish. When you have written your limericks, you could get into groups and have a limerick-telling session, either reading them out, or reciting them from memory.

8 WAYS OF LOOKING

Poetry doesn't only involve words on a page. It also involves new ways of looking.

In our day-to-day lives people, feelings, objects can become so familiar that we can stop noticing how special they really are. Poetry reminds us that there are many different ways of thinking about things and looking at them. This is how poetry helps us rediscover ourselves and the world around us.

Here is a poem based on the idea of different ways of looking:

SIX VIEWS OF A WATERFALL Gareth Owen

When the river threw itself off the cliff
It spun a twist of rope
So as not to lose touch with itself.

The river of a sudden
Tired of lying down between fields
And having the sky painted on its face
Stood up and was pleased.

Around the holy water where the miracle happened
They hollowed out a damp chapel
And glued green carpets on the wall to absorb the sound.
Every day someone brings fresh ferns.

We can see the silent film through the beaded curtain
There is interference on the vertical hold
And for a comedy there should be subtitles,
But the actors shout just the same.

Sometimes the river stays still
And children swim upstream.
After a time they lie down and walk away.

At home they have sardines for tea
And later go to bed.
While this is going on
The waterfall does what it always has done
And doesn't dream about people.

Divide into pairs or small groups. Choose two or three of these views of a waterfall and read them again. Then describe to each other the pictures that come into your mind as you read them.

Discuss anything you think is striking or unusual about how the poet has described the waterfall. Then report back to the rest of the class, giving your views on his 'views'.

MORE THINGS TO DO

As a class, decide on an object or idea to write about. You can continue the views of a waterfall, or you can choose a different idea, for example, the wind. Each person write one view of the object, then combine them with the views from the rest of the class to make one long poem. Finally, through class discussion, decide on the order of the views which you think is best. You could copy it out and mount it on the wall with illustrations. Here are some views of a waterfall which are written by pupils.

The water, like lemmings,
rushes towards the edge,
ending in tranquillity.

The water
is an old man with long, white hair,
plunging into the cavity below.

The waterlift
goes down to the bottom floor.

Somewhere
the knob is stuck on the shower.
It can never be turned off.

The waterfall is a waterwall.
Behind it is another land.

When woken from its sleep
The river is fresh, roaring down the rocks,
exercising itself.

As the river runs downstream
It gets careless
and slips and falls downstairs.

You can't teach a waterfall new things.
It shouts out that it knows
all it needs to know.

The pupils of 2HG, Bishopslea School

9 COUNTING THE WAYS AND THE WORDS

The poem below celebrates not ways of looking, but ways of touching something familiar.

FOURTEEN WAYS OF TOUCHING THE PETER George Macbeth

I
You can push
your thumb
in the
ridge
between his
shoulder-blades
to please him.

II
Starting
at its root,
you can let
his whole
tail
flow
through your hand.

III
Forming
a fist
you can let
him rub
his bone
skull
against it, hard.

IV
When he makes
bread,
you can lift
him
by his under
sides on your
knuckles.

V
In hot
weather
you can itch
the fur
under
his chin. He
likes that.

VI
At night
you can hoist
him
out of his bean-stalk,
sleepily
clutching
paper bags.

VII

Pressing
his head against
your cheek,
you can carry
him
in the dark,
safely.

VIII

In late Autumn
you can find
seeds
adhering
to his fur.
There are
plenty.

IX

You can prise
his jaws
open,
helping
any medicine
he won't
abide, go down.

X

You can touch
his
feet, only
if
he is relaxed.
He
doesn't like it.

XI

You can comb
spare thin
fur
from his coat,
so he won't
get
fur-ball.

XII

You can shake
his rigid
chicken-leg leg,
scouring his
hind-quarters
with his Vim
tongue.

XIII

Dumping
hot fish
on his plate, you can
fend
him off,
pushing
and purring.

XIV

You can have
him shrimp
along you,
breathing,
whenever
you want
to compose poems.

In pairs, discuss these questions.

a What is 'the Peter'? (There is a picture over the page, but don't look until you've answered the question.)

b Why has the poet called him 'the Peter', instead of simply Peter?

c How many words are there in each section of the poem? (Hyphenated words count as one.) How many lines are there in each section?

d How do these numbers relate to the poem as a whole?

Using numbers

The poem about the Peter is very carefully organised by numbers. Setting yourself a strict number of words and lines to use can be very helpful in writing a poem, making you concentrate upon using words in the most economical and effective way.

Here is a poem written by a pupil, which gives nine different views of the sky. The writer has chosen to use clear schemes with which to organise the poem. What is the target for lines and words per stanza?

NINE VIEWS OF THE SKY   Paul Scola

When the weather
changes, he wears
his different coats.

Time goes
so he slowly turns off
his torch.

A wide, deep, blue ocean
waiting
to be explored.

A gigantic space
waiting to be filled
by pollution.

Clouds with anger
get black
and let out tears.

He lights up
the world with
his bright lamp.

Shaving cream
is up there
floating around the air.

People fly straight
through him.
They just don't care.

He holds the white
diamond stars
in his hand.

MORE THINGS TO DO

There are endless possibilities for writing poems based on this idea of different ways of looking, or of doing something. For example, you could have:

Six views of school
Seven ways of making or losing a friend
Nine ways of doing (or not doing) your homework
Twenty-one views of a hedgehog

It's up to you!

Try this for yourself. On your own, in pairs or in small groups:

♦ Decide on the idea or object you are going to write about.
♦ Work out your numbers scheme. How many words and lines do you want in each stanza? What will the total number of stanzas be?
♦ Write the different views (or ways of doing something).
♦ Change the order of the stanzas in the way you think works best.

REMEMBER
With a poem you can open people's eyes and minds to new ways of looking, thinking and feeling.

---

10 NEAR RHYMES

> Roses are red,
> Cabbages are green,
> My face is funny
> But yours is a scream.

There are many other ways to rhyme apart from using full rhymes. A Near Rhyme happens when two words end with sounds which are close enough to be similar but which aren't exactly the same. Which words nearly rhyme in the chant above?

You can make near rhymes from consonants or vowels. Taking the word 'hat', full rhymes would be . . . cat, sat, mat . . .

To make near rhymes of 'hat' from consonants you change the vowel:

hat: near rhymes: hit, hot, hut, height . . .

To make near rhymes from the vowel you change one or both of the consonants:

hat: near rhymes: had, ham, has, can, map . . .

Near rhymes are sometimes called false rhymes, but this is misleading because they are not mistakes. They are part of daily conversation in phrases such as *dilly-dally*, li*fe-l*ine, *p*ie*ce-m*e*al*, *fl*o*tsam* and *j*e*tsam*, str*oke* of lu*ck* . . .

Near rhymes are also common in folk rhymes and playground chants. Get into pairs and read aloud the lines below, listening for the near rhymes. Discuss each example and say why the sounds are similar.

> Who gave you that jolly red nose?
> Cinnamon, Ginger, Nutmeg and Cloves.

> I pinch you, you can't pinch back,
> For I see a man in a white straw hat.

> Pin, pin, bring me luck,
> Because I stop to pick you up.

> Baby, baby bunting, cried for apple dumpling.

Off with the jackets,
Up with the sleeves.
Biff! Bang!
Down on your knees.

See my finger
See my thumb
See my fist –
You'd better run!

No more school, thank goodness for that!
Ha! Ha! Ha! I can go and slack!

Near rhymes are very effective whether you are writing rhyming poems or free-verse.

Read aloud the poem below which is based on a traditional rhyme.

THE MAN WHO WASN'T THERE   Brian Lee

Yesterday upon the stair
I met a man who wasn't there;
He wasn't there again today,
I wish, I wish, he'd go away.

I've seen his shapeless shadow-coat
Beneath the stairway, hanging about;
And outside, muffled in a cloak
The same colour as the dark;

I've seen him in a black, black suit
Shaking, under the broken light;
I've seen him swim across the floor
And disappear beneath the door;

And once, I almost heard his breath
Behind me, running up the path:
Inside, he leant against the wall,
And turned . . . and was no-one at all.

Yesterday upon the stair
I met a man who wasn't there;
He wasn't there again today,
I wish, I wish, he'd go away.

Look for the near rhymes in the poem. In pairs, prepare a reading of the poem for the rest of the class. Try to express the kind of atmosphere which you think the poem has.

MORE THINGS TO DO

1 To practise making near rhymes you can play 'Roaming Rhyming' in pairs, groups or as a class. Starting with a key word, each person in turn adds a near rhyme, by changing the consonant sounds, then the vowel sounds etc. A round of the game could go like this:

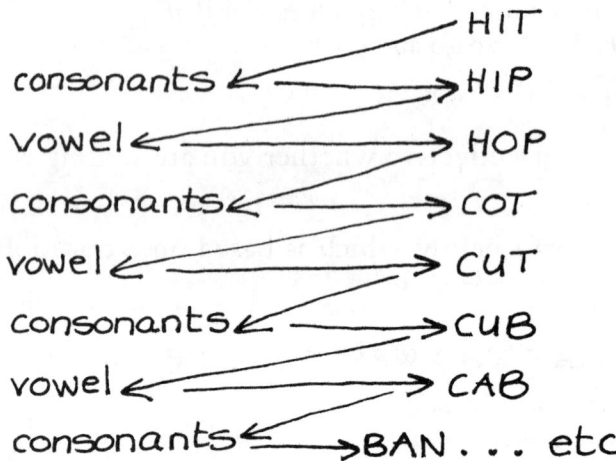

```
                                    ⟋ HIT
        consonants ⟵ ———————⟶ HIP
        vowel ⟵ ———————————⟶ HOP
        consonants ⟵ ——————⟶ COT
        vowel ⟵ ———————————⟶ CUT
        consonants ⟵ ——————⟶ CUB
        vowel ⟵ ——————————⟶ CAB
        consonants ⟵ ——⟶ BAN . . . etc
```

You could start by writing your near rhymes down and reading them out. Then when you get better at the game you could just say them. You are out if you make a full rhyme!

Here are some key words you could use:

   lock   doll   drain   bite   grass   cup   bet   sip

2 Tell each other any playground chants you can remember. Write them down. Visit a primary school near you and ask the children to tell you the rhymes they know. Collect the rhymes and make a wall display of them. Look out for any near rhymes.

3 Interview some adults about the poems, rhymes and chants they remember from their early childhood. You could tape-record the interviews and write out some of the poems you hear.

4 Make up a playground chant of your own. You could use one of the following topics which are common in traditional chants:

   food   ghosts   nonsense   nicknames   luck   school

REMEMBER
When you are writing a rhyming poem, you never have to use a word you don't want, for the sake of making a rhyme.

---

11 OPPOSITES

The poem below is organised through the repetition of the phrases 'What I love about . . .' and 'What I hate about . . .'. In pairs, read it aloud, one person reading the 'love' lines, the other reading the 'hate' lines.

A VIEW OF THINGS   Edwin Morgan

what I love about dormice is their size
what I hate about rain is its sneer
what I love about the Bratach Gorm is its unflappability
what I hate about scent is its smell
what I love about newspapers is their etaoin shrdl
what I hate about philosophy is its pursed lip
what I love about Rory is his old grouse
what I hate about Pam is her pinkie
what I love about semi-precious stones is their preciousness
what I hate about diamonds is their mink
what I love about poetry is its ion engine
what I hate about dogs is their setae
what I love about love is its porridge spoon
what I hate about hate is its eyes
what I love about hate is its salts
what I hate about love is its dog
what I love about Hank is his string vest
what I hate about the twins is their three gloves
what I love about Mabel is her teeter
what I hate about gooseberries is their look, feel, smell, and taste
what I love about the world is its shape
what I hate about a gun is its lock, stock and barrel
what I love about bacon-and-eggs is its unpredictability
what I hate about derelict buildings is their reluctance to disintegrate
what I love about a cloud is its unpredictability
what I hate about you, chum, is your china
what I love about many waters is their inability to quench love

The writer has mentioned all sorts of things in the poem. The pattern of statements which he uses is repetitive and predictable, but what he notices about each thing is unexpected and surprising. Pick four lines, two beginning with 'What I love about . . . .'. and two beginning with 'What I hate about . . . .'. In your pairs, discuss what you found surprising in them and why you think the poet chose to notice those details about the things he included.

Are there any lines which you do not understand? Discuss them and try to decide what the poet might mean.

MORE THINGS TO DO

1 Choose four things included in the poem above. Arrange them into a list following the 'What I love about/What I hate about' pattern. Complete each line in your own way. For example, for dormice you might say

> What I love about dormice is their twitchy noses

2 You could use the love/hate idea, but choosing your own objects as well as the details about them:

> What I love about . . . . . . is . . . . . .
> What I hate about . . . . . . is . . . . . . etc

or you could use other opposites, such as

> What makes me happy . . . is . . .
> What makes me sad . . . is . . .
>
> In the country I feel . . .
> In the city I feel . . .
>
> A good thing about . . . is . . .
> A bad thing about . . . is . . .
> A good thing was . . .
> A bad thing was . . .

To write your 'opposites' poem,

♦ Write a list of the objects (actions, events, people etc) you want to include.
♦ Complete each line, thinking carefully about the most important detail for you.

REMEMBER
Try to make your lists surprising and interesting, so that anyone who reads your poem won't quite know what to expect next.

12 ACROSTICS

We all know that when we read the English language we move our eyes from left to right along horizontal lines. (You've just done this. You're doing it now.) There are many other languages, though, which don't work in this way. This is a sample of Hebrew writing. To read this you go from right to left, the opposite way to English.

בְּהָיִיץ הָ'ה שׁוֹתֵק וְחֹשֶׁק , וְרוּחַ נָשְׁבָה דֶרֶךְ הַחַלּוֹן הַפָּתִיחַ .

In Arabic, too, you read from right to left. When you open a book, you would start at what would be the back page for books in English!

كان البيت ساكنا و مظلما و سبّ
الريح خلال الشبّاك المفتوح .

In Chinese not only do you read from right to left. You also move from top to bottom, in other words vertically.

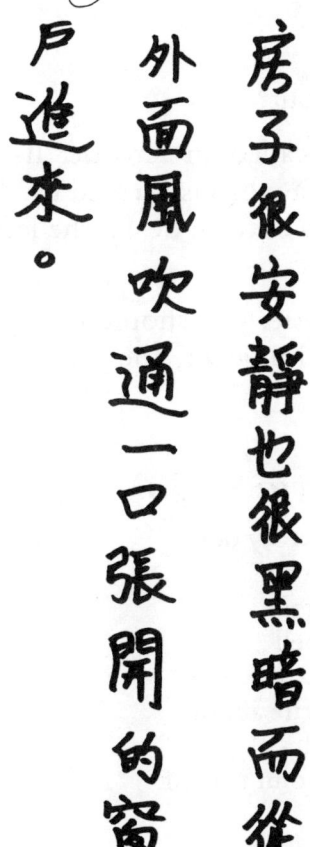

Do you know of any other languages which are read in ways other than horizontally (across the page) from left to right? Make a list, describing how the eyes move over the words in each case.

There is a special type of poem which works by being read from left to right and from top to bottom. Carefully read the poem below.

Crawls like a miniature ocean
Arriving at an unknown destination
Tenderly feels round a leaf,
Every contact is brief, as if entering a naked flame.
Repeatedly moves its short legs
Purposefully arches then straightens,
Ignorant of the prodding hand,
Leans, and falls, to land on a leaf below.
Lazy, yet possessing a delightful beauty,
Adrift in a world of dizziness –
Red stripes like blood-stained gashes on its back.

Mark Nathan

What is this poem about?

This type of poem is called an acrostic. Its special feature is that when you read downwards, a word is formed by the first letter of each line. So by reading from top to bottom down the left-hand side of the poem you can find out its subject.

When writing an acrostic, you should not split words at the end of lines. In this next example, however, the writer has deliberately broken that rule for a joke:

AN ACROSTIC   Roger McGough

A favourite literary devi
Ce is the one whe
Re the first letter
Of each line spell
S out the subject the poe
T wishes to write about.
I must admit, I
Can't see the point myself.

In many ways acrostics are like riddles, except that the answer is given when the poem is read downwards. But the main reply to Roger McGough's poem above is that acrostics are about playing with words to discover the effects you can create.

Here are some acrostics written by pupils.

Flickering on the walls
Indigo, yellow and red.
Reflections of each tiny flame,
Every shadow dances.
Light so bright it lingers still
In my cottage room.
Ghostly spirits loom.
Heat so strong it leaves
Tingles in my toes.

Caroline Needham

Softly the flakes fall,
Nothing seems to stir.
Over the world a thick blanket lies
White, soft and crispy light.

Caroline Needham

Frontiers contain
Unknown destinations.
Travel into space
U.F.O.s?
Return?
Energy must be found!

Jenny Sykes

Vigorous I am not
I am as lazy as can be
Very lazy
Indeed I'm lazy
Ever so lazy
Not vigorous, not me.

My name is Vivien
A really awful name
Really an awful name. Even
Kate is better than Vivien.
Of all the names in the world I got
Vivien.
It's not that bad I suppose, but I still
Cringe at the thought of that name!

Vivien Markovic

Slowly I slip into a world of
Lovely, never
Ending dreams. Lying there for
Ever
Peacefully under the covers
Ignoring all the
Noise. One thing I look forward to is
Going to bed at night.

Kate Noble

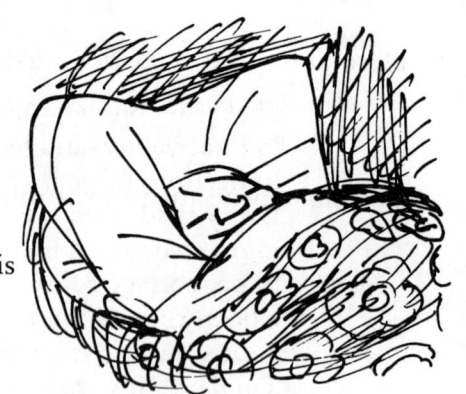

All the lovely sunshine,
Underneath the trees
Sitting in the shade
Taking in the breeze.
Riding on a pony,
Along a dusty track
Lying there
In the privacy of the outback
Alone.

Melanie Greyson

MORE THINGS TO DO

1 Try writing an acrostic. You could start with a simple idea such as your name, or the name of any of the following things: an insect, an animal, a bird, a town, a country, a month, a season, a fruit, a musical instrument, a television programme, a film, a sport, a team, a pop/film star.

> **REMEMBER**
> ♦ Acrostics can have a regular rhythm and rhyme (as in some of the poems above) but it is ~   od idea to use free-verse, because then you can concentrate on making the acrostic.
> ♦ The first letter of each line is part of another word when read downwards.
> ♦ Do not split words at the end of the lines.
> ♦ Avoid using the word spelt out from top to bottom anywhere else in your poem.

2 When you have completed one or two of these suggestions, you could try a more unusual idea, phrase or theme, perhaps using more than one word, e.g. W A R A N D P E A C E.

Try whatever catches your imagination.

13 FREE-VERSE POEMS

In Book One, Unit 8, we worked on free-verse poetry. This unit contains some more examples of free-verse poems.

NORTHERN LINE   Tom Pickard

a ten-year-old boy
            with glasses
and scraggy
            red hair
keeps falling off
            to sleep
he counts
            the cooling ovens
they're all around
                a forest
    of smoking towers
by him
        a white bag
with blue letters
LEEDS UNITED
            and in gold
THE CHAMPIONS

is that your team?
aye!
    who d'you support
        newcastle?
            I don't suppose you
want to talk about
        last saturday!
I didn't

Why do you think the writer did not want to talk about the previous Saturday?

The poem above records some interesting observations, but what makes them even more effective is the way the poem is set out. What do you notice about the way the words are arranged on the page?

How does the poet make some words stand out? Why does he do this?

Choose some words or phrases which you particularly notice and discuss where they are placed in the poem.

Here is a free-verse poem by a second-year girl which uses line divisions in a similar way to *Northern Line*.

THE WATERFALL   Julia Walker

Gleaming gently, slowly
      towards the open skies
rippling along without force or
               anger
trickling over and against the stones
but suddenly and without warning
  leaping
    thrashing,
      the water bursts away
and into all hidden
        directions
away it goes
    to uncover the sleepy world and
to wrestle with quietness
      throwing itself against the banks
       disappearing slowly away
no-one knows where
no-one cares

By dividing the lines you show where you want the pauses to be, so punctuation becomes less important.

Here are some more free-verse poems written by pupils.

Get into pairs. Read them aloud and then choose one to discuss in more detail. When you have done this report back to the class on the poem you chose. Describe what it was about and your reaction to it. Did the layout help the effect of the poem? If you feel it did, explain how.

WHAT I KNOW   Susan Jones

it's nice sitting here
I can feel the breeze
  brushing against me
it's so desolate and so wonderful
  no-one is as happy as me
I can hear the waves
      rushing to meet me
  the beauty of
        emptiness
    all around me

no sin can survive here
no-one can feel unhappy
I cry
    with joy
when a tiny seagull flies away
        across the water
I don't know why
I suppose it is because
I am alive
        to see such things
and I know I am lucky
and I know I can never feel
    or be
        lonely

THE SCHOOLBOY   Mark O'Grady

Big, strong, scruffy thing
Never had a wash in a month of Sundays.
Fist like iron, head like wood,
Born daft, still is daft.
Holes in the back of his trousers.
Tells big whoppers.
Said he went to Spain,
    walks fifteen miles before breakfast.
Some whoppers he tells.
Ask him the time:
    'Five to ten, no six to nine.'
Ask him one and one:
    'Six.'
How do trees become trees?
    'People build trees.'
No-one is as daft as him.

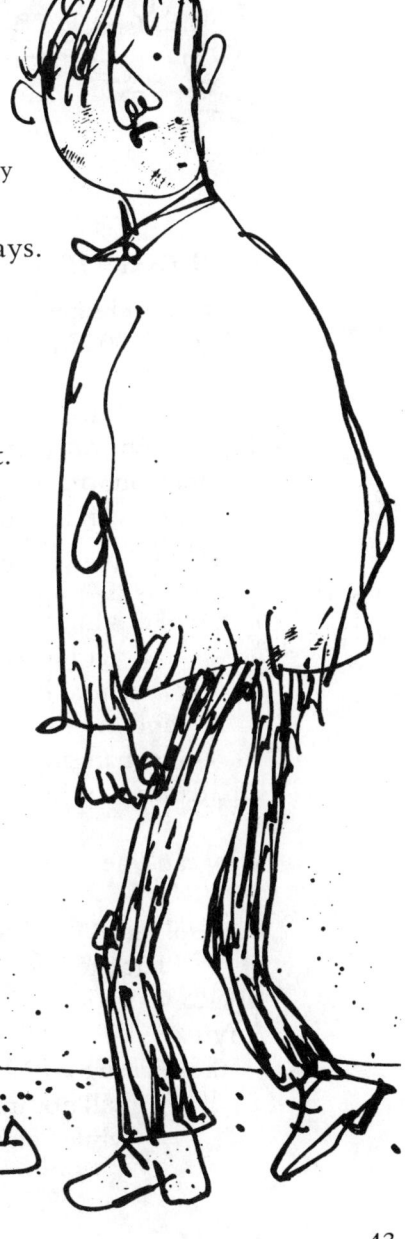

FEELING TIRED   Anne Hicks

Why should I get up?
It's only 8.30. Anyway
               the clock's wrong.
Well, I'm almost certain it is.
The curtains can stay closed.
I'll block out the busy day
    for just a bit longer.
I'll get up
         soon
I know I ought to
        but yet I feel so tired
my eyes seem to be weighing me down
        and my limbs are
               hanging heavily upon my body.
Oh, damn it, why does the milkman
              have to wake me up?
Why can't he rattle his milk bottles
                somewhere else?
I get up! I go
      back to bed.
My tea was cold and Mum had let the fire go out.
Anyway
    the exciting whirl of the morning
        will not miss me
        while I stay in bed.

SCRUMPING APPLES   Martin Bonner

We entered the garden from the highest and most dangerous wall
     possible,
With pieces of glass set in the top.
The other two climbed over first with ease.
I was sure I could do the same as them,
But, when I got up to the wall and dug in my shoe tips
     and my weak skin clutched at the coarse brick,
Then my eyes viewed the glass and
I realised I was defeated.
I imagined my friends to be away by then,
     across the boggy fields that I knew lay beyond.
I called out to them in a shallow voice.
They were gone!
The trust and confidence that had been built up between us was also
     gone.
Deep down I was furious with myself for not regarding my
     inner beliefs of the characters that existed within the faces.
The fruits of my mind had been stolen from their very innards.
Determined for revenge, I went round to the front
     and told on them.

THE LAST MOMENTS   Kim Raine

He sat beside her
I'm sure he knew
She was in her last moments
Her breathing deepened
Her chest moved quickly
Her fur was hot
  A big thud
She was on her side
He licked her gently
She was one minute dead
  and still very warm
I held her limp body
  and her floppy head

I cradled her close
  to my warmth
I kissed her forehead
  and stroked her ears
Her eyes were fixed
  and very wide
He sat still
  beside the empty space
The loss we shared
  greater for him than me
For I wasn't a rabbit
  like he

MY FIRST FRIEND   Robert Jones

My first friend,
  the milkman,
        Curly.
That's what he called me.
I had all curly hair then
I started calling him Curly
   and it's his nickname now.
But
   he's no curls.
I used to peep round the fence.
'Curly!' I'd shout.
He'd shout back:
    'You're the one with the curls!'
He'd knock on our door for Mum to pay.
I'd answer the door.
He'd put his hand on my head
And say:
    'Son, I like your curls.'
I was glad somebody did,
   a friend.
Mum had all my curls cut off.
Curly was curly all on his own,
But
I was still his friend.

MORE THINGS TO DO

1 Try writing three or four lines on any subject. Then shift the layout around for different kinds of effect. For example, the three lines below about rain at night could be rearranged in different ways.

> Just when I was floating into a calm sea of sleep
> The wind came rudely smacking against the window pane.
> A thousand footsteps marched inside my head.

The lines could be set out like this:

> Just when I was
>   floating
> into a calm sea of sleep
> the wind came
> rudely smacking against the window pane.
> A thousand
>   footsteps
>   marched
>   inside
>   my head.

or like this:

> Just when I was floating
>   into a calm sea of sleep
> the wind came
>   rudely smacking
> against the window pane.
> A thousand footsteps marched inside my head.

In pairs, discuss the effect of different kinds of layout for your lines, and say which you prefer and why.

2 Write a free-verse poem of your own. If you're not sure what to write about, your teacher will give you a list of themes to choose from. You can use a theme as the starting point for your poem by following the stages below.

♦ Choose a theme to write about. The theme is not the title of the poem.
♦ Jot down particular ideas, situations and memories which come into your mind in connection with the theme you have chosen.
♦ Choose one of the ideas to develop into a poem and write a first draft.
♦ Decide on the kind of layout you want and then go through your poem and put in the line divisions where you feel they work best.
♦ Rework your first draft into a final version and write it out.

REMEMBER
You are free to set the poem out just as you wish and the layout can be a useful way of giving your words more impact.

---

14 A PUN MY WORD!

Many modern riddles and jokes are based on words which have two meanings. Below are some jokes which work like this, but the questions and answers have been mixed up. Match the answers to the questions then try the jokes out on a partner.

Which animal never fights fair?

How do you write a letter to a fish?

What is a prickly pear? Why did the biscuit cry?

What sort of tiles can't be stuck on a wall?

What do you get if you lie under a cow?

What do you stuff dead parrots with?

Why did the lobster blush?

A pat on the head.

Reptiles. Because the seaweed.

Polyfilla. A cheetah. Two porcupines.

Because its mother had been a wafer so long.

Drop it a line.

Playing with double meanings is called punning, or making a pun. Get into pairs. Each person pick three of the jokes above and explain to your partner the two meanings being played with in each of the jokes you have chosen.

Puns aren't just used in jokes and riddles. They are a very common and basic type of wordplay and are found in many forms of writing, including advertising slogans, graffiti, book or film titles, newspaper headlines and poetry. They are usually deliberate, but they can be accidental, as in the following examples of actual headlines opposite.

Divide into pairs. In turns, explain to your partner the intended and unintended meaning of each headline.

Threatening letters –man asks for long sentence

Scotsman

PASSENGERS HIT BY CANCELLED TRAINS

Manchester Evening News

Spare our trees—they break wind

THE whole character of Bognor Regis as a holiday resort could change if a plantation of 60ft.-high trees at the west end of the town is cut down for housing development.

This warning was given yesterday by Mr. Edmond Venables, chairman of Bognor branch of the Wild Life Association.

Said Mr. Venables: "The trees are very densely planted and give a terrific amount of protection from the south-west and westerly gales. A 60ft.-high tree can break wind for up to one mile.

Evening Argus

Crash courses for private pilots

Daily Telegraph

THREE BATTERED IN FISH SHOP
Man gaoled for assault

Evening News

Bodies in the garden are a plant says wife

Hong Kong Standard

The familiar pattern of a 'Knock! Knock!' joke is based on a pun. In this case the pun is always made on a NAME. Here are some examples:

Knock! Knock!
Who's there?
Francis.
Francis who?
France is on the other side of the Channel.

Knock! Knock!
Who's there?
Wayne.
Wayne who?
Wayne is coming down; I want my umbrella.

Knock! Knock!
Who's there?
Tina.
Tina who?
Tina baked beans.

Knock! Knock!
Who's there?
Lemmy.
Lemmy who?
Lemme in at once!

Knock! Knock!
Who's there?
Carmen.
Carmen who?
Carmen see for yourself.

Do you know any 'Knock! Knock!' jokes? If you do, tell them to a partner.

MORE THINGS TO DO

1 Though 'Knock! Knock!' jokes aren't poems, they can be linked with poems because they involve playing with words and because, like many poems, they follow a clear pattern.

- There are always 5 lines.
- The first two lines of the joke are always the same:

Knock! Knock!
Who's there?

- The third line is the name.
- The fourth line is the name plus the question 'Who?'.
- The fifth line turns the name into an unexpected pun.

Try to make up some 'Knock! Knock!' jokes of your own. The parts of the joke which stay the same are shown below. Copy them out and fill in the blank spaces with your own ideas:

Knock! Knock!
Who's there?
——————.
———— who?
————————————.

Here are some names which you might find useful.

Ida   Eva   Eve   Ivor   Ivan   Ed   Edna   Etta   Carrie   Doug
Gustave   Ben   Wilma   Annie   Warren   Dustin   Harriet   Mark
Laura   Lois   Russell   Adam   Donna   Betty   Alan   Isabel
Lulu   Otto   Justin   Tara   Heidi   Lorraine   Robin   Shirley
Tony   Wanda   Toya   Haydn   Hugo   Orson   Andrew   Saul
Rex   Tanya   Bing   Mona   Mustapha   Doris   Titus   Eileen
Gail   Lori   Ima   Neil   Rhoda   Yul

15 PUNS AND POEMS

Which kind of tree grows from words?
Poetree.

Double meanings can be used seriously in poetry and other writing. This poem uses a pun in a serious way.

JAILBIRD   Vernon Scannell

His plumage is dun,
Talons long but blunt.
His appetite is indiscriminate.
He has no mate and sleeps alone
In a high nest built of brick and steel.
He sings at night
A long song, sad and silent.
He cannot fly.

The pun is in the title of the poem. A jailbird is someone who is in prison, but the writer uses the expression to develop an image of a prisoner as a caged bird. The poet takes the ordinary word and explores it to find a new meaning.

Nevertheless, though puns can be serious, nowadays they are more often used humorously. A change of spelling is sometimes all that is needed to make a pun; e.g. 'I spent a holiday in grease.' (It was very uncomfortable!)

A pun can be the main idea in a poem, or just a small part of a poem. The following poems are all based on, or contain puns. Read them and see if you can spot the play with meanings.

RADI   Anon

Radi was a circus lion,
Radi was a woman hater.
Radi had a lady trainer,
Radiator.

What are the two meanings suggested by the last word in this rhyme?

FOOLISH QUESTIONS   William Cole

Where can a man buy a cap for his knee?
Or a key for the lock of his hair?
And can his eyes be called at school?
I would think – there are pupils there.
What jewels are found in the crown of his head,
And who walks on the bridge of his nose?
Can he use, in building the roof of his mouth,
The nails on the ends of his toes?
Can the crook of his elbow be sent to jail–
If it can, well, then what did it do?
And how does he sharpen his shoulder blades?
I'll be hanged if I know – do you?
Can he sit in the shade of the palm of his hand,
And beat time with the drum of his ear?
Can the calf of his leg eat the corn of his toe?
There's something pretty strange around here!

How many puns can you find in this poem? Discuss them with a partner.

EYE SORE   Roger McGough

I saw
a building
soar
into the sky

making
the sky's
eye
sore.

There are several meanings being played with here, based on just one phrase. How many can you discover? The poem makes a serious point. What is it?

The next poem is a conversation between two people. Get into pairs and read it aloud. Person A asks the questions and B gives the answers, but B finishes off the poem with the last question.

RABBITING ON   Kit Wright

Where did you go?
Oh . . . nowhere much.

What did you see?
Oh . . . rabbits and such.

Rabbits? What else?
Oh . . . a rabbit hutch.

What sort of rabbits?
What sort? Oh . . . small.

What sort of hutch?
Just a hutch, that's all.

But what did it look like?
Like a rabbit hutch.

Well, what was in it?
Small rabbits and such.

I worried about you
While you were gone.

Why don't you stop
Rabbiting on?

What is the pun in this poem?

Adrian Henri based the poem below on a joke that a boy told him:

What do you get if you cross a hyena with an Oxo cube?
A laughing stock.

SQUARE MEAL   Adrian Henri

He kept a pet hyena
And then he bought a flock
He fed them all on Oxo cubes
And made a laughing stock.

Why did Adrian Henri call the poem 'Square Meal'?

This is a poem by a pupil.

PLUG IT   Alison Barry

It's made of earth, yet
   pretty solid
And it's a real live wire,
In fact the connection
   can be quite shocking!
The three copper pins
   are metal towers,
Which supply powers,
   via wires
Through adapters and fuses
   and screws,
And at the flick of a
   switch
Electricity will socket
   to you!

Watt are the puns in this poem?

MORE THINGS TO DO

1 Make a collection of your favourite jokes based on puns. Memorise as many as you can to tell to other people, but don't tell too many or your puns could become a punishment.

2 Try to make up some jokes or riddles of your own which use puns. Your joke should be in the form of a question and an answer. For your joke to work, your question should suggest one meaning and the answer should suggest two meanings. Here are two examples:

Which are the strongest fish?   Mussels.
What do windows suffer from?   Window panes.

3 Write some punning poems of your own. They don't have to be very long. A good way to do this is by taking a joke which contains a pun and using that as the idea for your poem, as Adrian Henri did in his poem 'Square Meal'. If you choose to write your poem in this way, you can use any of the jokes in this unit, or jokes of your own. It's up to you whether or not your poem has a regular rhyme and rhythm.

4 Look out for puns which crop up in newspaper headlines or magazines. (The funniest are the ones that are accidental.) Make a class display of them.

5 In small groups, have a joke-telling, poem-speaking session using preposterous puns.

16 PERFORMING POEMS

Reading silently to yourself is one way of experiencing poetry. But many poems really come alive and are fully enjoyed when we speak them and when we hear them spoken. All the poems in this unit are presented for you to read aloud and to perform.

Get into pairs. First of all, read the poem below silently to yourself. Then read the poem aloud to your partner. Finally, listen to your partner's reading of the poem.

THE SONG OF THE WHALE   Kit Wright

Heaving mountain in the sea,
Whale, I heard you
Grieving.

Great whale, crying for your life,
Crying for your kind, I knew
How we would use
Your dying:

Lipstick for our painted faces,
Polish for our shoes.

Tumbling mountain in the sea,
Whale, I heard you
Calling.

Bird-high notes, keening, soaring:
At their edge a tiny drum
Like a heartbeat.

We would make you
Dumb.

In the forest of the sea,
Whale, I heard you
Singing,

Singing to your own kind.
We'll never let you be.
Instead of life we choose

Lipstick for our painted faces,
Polish for our shoes.

Were there any differences in your appreciation of the poem between reading it silently and hearing it read aloud?

Did the way you read the poem out loud differ from the way your partner read it? If so what were the differences?

Are there any parts of this poem which would gain by being read by more than one voice?

Poems are often read aloud by one person, but they can be even more exciting when read by a group of people. In pairs or small groups, read aloud all the poems below. Then pick one poem from the unit (including the one above) to prepare for a performance to the rest of the class.

When you have chosen a poem, read it again once or twice, listening to the words carefully. Discuss the ideas and feelings which you think the poem expresses. What do you think was the poet's intention in writing the poem? What message or feeling do you wish to bring out in your reading?

Then organise your reading carefully. You can do this by dividing the poem into parts and thinking about the following points:

- Who will read each part?
- Will some parts be read by more than one person, e.g. by pairs or groups of speakers?
- Pay particular attention to the rhythm. What will be the pace of your reading? Will it be brisk and lively, or slow?
- Is there a regular rhyme scheme in the poem? If there is not, are there any occasional rhymes which you might want to bring out? (e.g. you may have noticed that there are several occasional rhymes in 'The Song of the Whale')
- Are there parts of the poem or particular words where you could emphasise the sounds of the letters?
- Are there any simple actions or movements which you could do to help in your performance?
- What tone of voice will you use for particular words and phrases?
- Does the punctuation give you any clues as to how the words could be read?
- Above all, what is the general mood and atmosphere that you are trying to create with your performance?

GHOSTS IN OUR SUBURBAN HOMES   Jan Dean

The creaking of a wicker chair
When something unseen settles there.
It's ghosts, ss, ss, ss,
It's ghosts.
Mad wardrobes swinging in the night,
A flicker at the edge of sight,
It's ghosts, ss, ss, ss,
It's ghosts.
The rocker rocks. The curtains sigh.
Out of the corner of your eye
The solid darkness passes by,
It's ghosts!

They spread themselves along the wall,
Shadows with shadows haunt the hall,
A great grey silent waterfall
Of ghosts!

Come midnight, watch the stair-
Tread sink with no foot there.
It's ghosts, ss, ss, ss,
It's ghosts.
A thousand thousand whispering souls
Mass quietly behind small holes.
A million slither through the cracks
Behind the door, behind our backs,
Insinuating warm as wax
Are ghosts!

And in the silence of the moon,
The silver silence of the moon,
The ghosts release a silent tune
To rise like steam from some sad tomb.
The soundless song of frozen skies,
The ice of unsung lullabies,
Wordless as the frosted eyes
Of ghosts.

Ghosts in our suburban homes.
Ghosts in our suburban homes.
Ghosts, ss, ss, ss,
Ghosts.

THE LONGEST JOURNEY IN THE WORLD   Michael Rosen

'Last one into bed
has to switch out the light.'
It's just the same every night.
There's a race.
I'm ripping off my trousers and shirt,
he's kicking off his shoes and socks.

'My sleeve's stuck.'
'This button's too big for its button-hole.'
'Have you hidden my pyjamas?'
'Keep your hands off mine.'

If you win
you get where it's safe
before the darkness comes –
but if you lose
if you're last
you know what you've got coming up is
the journey from the light switch to the bed.
It's the Longest Journey in the World.

'You're last tonight,' my brother says.
And he's right.

There is nowhere so dark
as that room in that moment
after I've switched out the light.

There is nowhere so full of dangerous things,
things that love dark places,
things that breathe only when you breathe
and hold their breath when I hold mine.

So I have to say:
'I'm not scared.'
That face grinning in the pattern on the wall,
Isn't a face –
'I'm not scared.'
The prickle on the back of my neck
is only the label on my pyjama jacket –
'I'm not scared.'
That moaning-moaning is nothing
but water in a pipe –
'I'm not scared.'

Everything's going to be just fine
as soon as I get into that bed of mine.
Such a terrible shame
it's always the same
it takes so long
it takes so long
it takes so long
to get there.
From the light switch
to my bed
it's the Longest Journey in the World.

LEAVES   Ted Hughes

Who's killed the leaves?

Me, says the apple, I've killed them all.
Fat as a bomb or a cannonball
I've killed the leaves.

Who sees them drop?

Me, says the pear, they will leave me all bare
So all the people can point and stare.
I see them drop.

Who'll catch their blood?

Me, me, me, says the marrow, the marrow.
I'll get so rotund that they'll need a wheelbarrow.
I'll catch their blood.

Who'll make their shroud?

Me, says the swallow, there's just time enough
Before I must pack all my spools and be off.
I'll make their shroud.

Who'll dig their grave?

Me, says the river, with the power of the clouds
A brown deep grave I'll dig under my floods.
I'll dig their grave.

Who'll be their parson?

Me, says the crow, for it is well-known
I study the bible right down to the bone.
I'll be their parson.

Who'll be chief mourner?

Me, says the wind, I will cry through the grass
The people will pale and go cold when I pass.
I'll be chief mourner.

Who'll carry the coffin?

Me, says the sunset, the whole world will weep
To see me lower it into the deep.
I'll carry the coffin.

Who'll sing a psalm?

Me, says the tractor, with my gear grinding grottle
I'll plough up their stubble and sing through my throttle.
I'll sing the psalm.

Who'll toll the bell?

Me, says the robin, my song in October
Will tell the still gardens the leaves are over.
I'll toll the bell.

HEALTH FANATIC   John Cooper Clarke

around the block against the clock
tick tock tick tock tick tick tock
running out of breath running out of socks
rubber on the road flippety-flop
non-skid agility chop chop
no time to hang about
work out health fanatic work out

crack of dawn lifting weights
tell-tale heart reverberates
high in polyunsaturates
low in polysaturates
the duke of edinburgh's award awaits
it's a man's life
he's a health fanatic so was his wife

a one-man war against decay
enjoys himself the hard way
allows himself a mars a day
how old am I what do I weigh
punch me there does it hurt no way
running on the spot don't get too hot
he's a health fanatic that's why not

running in the traffic jam taking in the lead
he gets hyper-activity never goes to bed
deep down he'd like to kick it in the head
they'll regret it when they're dead
there's more to life than fun
'cos he's a health fanatic he's got to run

beans greens tangerines
and low cholesterol margarines
his limbs are loose his teeth are clean
he's a high-octane fresh-air fiend
you've got to admit he's keen
well what can you do but be impressed
he's a health fanatic give it a rest

shadow boxing punch the wall
one-a-side football
what's the score one all
could have been a copper too small
could have been a jockey too tall
knees up knees up head the ball
nervous energy makes him tick
he's a health fanatic he makes you sick

'The Magic Tennis-Ball' by Roger McGough is a series of 3 poems plus an introduction. Like the rest of the poems in this unit, it is particularly effective when read aloud. Here are some suggestions which could be useful for performing this poem.

♦ The tennis-match poems, Number One and Number Three, are best read by two people, one person reading the words on the left of the page, the other person reading the words on the right. This gives the impression of the ball going backwards and forwards over the net.
♦ In the middle section concerning the Gallant Knight and the Lady Elinor, the stanzas can be read solo, while the chorus of fol de rols can be read by two people or more.

THE MAGIC TENNIS-BALL

(A Mystery in Three Poems)

Characters in order of appearance:

Tom
Me
The Gallant Knight
Lady Elinor
The Wicked Baron

NUMBER ONE

each	time
Tom	(aged
ten)	and
I	play
ten	nis
he	whacks
the	
high	over
the	net
and	right
out	of
the	court

NUMBER TWO

In armour bright
A gallant knight
Did journey through the meadow
To free the maiden
That he loved
And kill the Baron dead-o

Fol de rol, Fol de rol,
And kill the Baron dead-o.

On steed, milk-white
All day and night
In sunshine and in shadow
He journeyed long
And sang a song
For he was a handsome lad-o

Fol de rol, Fol de rol,
For he was a handsome lad-o.

Castle in sight
Our gallant knight
Did canter through the meadow
When a tennis-ball
Flew o'er the wall
And hit him on the head-o

Fol de rol, Fol de rol,
And hit him on the head-o.

'Gadzooks,' he cried
The stallion shied
Then galloped off arpeggio
He tried in vain
To hold the rein
But fell into a hedgerow

Fol de rol, Fol de rol,
But fell into a hedgerow.

Fair Elinor
Rolled on the floor
Laughing like a drain. 'Oh,
What a wimple
He must be simple,
If he wants my hand I'll say no.'

Fol de rol, Fol de rol,
If he wants my hand I'll say no.

The Baron roared
And waved his sword
Staggered helplessly, 'Ho-Ho-Ho.'
Till o'er he keeled
And dropped his shield
And broke his little toe-o

Fol de rol, Fol de rol,
And broke his little toe-o.

No sorrier sight
Than a buckled knight
Jeered at by damsel and foe. So
Cursing them all
He picked up the ball
And gave one almighty throw-o

Fol de rol, Fol de rol,
And gave one almighty throw-o.

NUMBER THREE

it	lands
back	on
the	court
so	we
can	con
tin	ue
our	game
Good	Knight.

'The Magic Tennis-Ball' has the subtitle 'A Mystery in Three Poems'. Part of the mystery is the way the poems are linked. The secret is that the connection is made through a pun (see Unit 14). Can you discover which word is used as the pun to connect the three poems? (A clue is that it is the name for the type of area you play tennis on.) The poem also ends with another pun. What is it?

MORE THINGS TO DO

1 You could practise reading aloud the poem you have chosen until you know the words off by heart. This isn't as difficult as you might think because the rhythm and rhymes (where there are any) help your memory. Then instead of reading your poem, you can recite it, which gives you even more freedom in your performance.

2 As a class, you could organise your own poetry show. You could perform the poems in this unit, or, if you wish, use your own choice of poems instead. You could put on your poetry show for other classes, other years, or, if you're feeling confident, for an assembly in front of the whole school. You could even take it on tour to other schools!

AN ANTHOLOGY

An anthology of poems is a collection of poems which are written by different people. This anthology contains poems for further reading, work and enjoyment. But this collection is only my choice. As time goes on you can choose your own poems and make up your own anthology. You can do this either by writing down the titles of the poems you like (and the titles of the books where you found them) at the back of your exercise book, or in a notebook, or you can have a special exercise book in which you copy out poems that you like to keep and to read in the future. Then, in time, you will have your own anthology which you will be able to read and enjoy and which might also tell you something about yourself. So keep your eyes, ears and minds open, because you can find poems anywhere.

Contents

I LIKE THAT STUFF

Lovers lie around in it.
Broken glass is found in it
Grass
I like that stuff

Tuna fish get trapped in it
Legs come wrapped in it
Nylon
I like that stuff

Eskimos and tramps chew it
Madame Tussaud gave status to it
Wax
I like that stuff

Elephants get sprayed with it
Scotch is made with it
Water
I like that stuff

Clergy are dumbfounded by it
Bones are surrounded by it
Flesh
I like that stuff

Harps are strung with it
Mattresses are sprung with it
Wire
I like that stuff

Cigarettes are lit by it
Pensioners get happy when they sit by it
Fire
I like that stuff

Dankworth's alto is made of it, most of it,
Scoobdedoo is composed of it
Plastic
I like that stuff

Man made fibres and raw materials
Old rolled gold and breakfast cereals
Platinum linoleum
I like that stuff

Skin on my hands
Hair on my head
Toenails on my feet
And linen on my bed

Well I like that stuff
Yes I like that stuff
    The earth
Is made of earth
    And I like that stuff

Adrian Mitchell

FISH

Fish
are not
very bright
not
by my
standards.
They
never had any
reason to grow
brains. For
one thing
it's hard
to read
under water and
the paper gets too wet
to handle and
there isn't the light and
fins let books slip and you'd
have to hold the
pen in your mouth.
People
who say
'A school of fish'
are
taking
advantage of
their limited
intelligence to poke cruel
fun.

You let
fish be.

Or eat them.

Ivor Cutler

FRIENDSHIP POEMS

(i)   There's good mates and bad mates
        'Sorry to keep you waiting' mates
    Cheap skates and wet mates
        The ones you end up hating mates
    Hard mates and fighting mates
        Witty and exciting mates
    Mates you want to hug
        And mates you want to clout
    Ones that get you into trouble
        And ones that get you out.

(ii)   Two's company
    One's lonely.

(iii) I'm a fish out of water
    I'm two left feet
    On my own and lonely
    I'm incomplete

    I'm boots without laces
    I'm jeans without the zip
    I'm lost, I'm a zombie
    I'm a dislocated hip.

(iv) When you're young
    Love sometimes confuses
    It clouds the brain
    And blows the fuses
    How often during those tender years
    You just can't see the wood for the tears.

Roger McGough

CITY LIGHTS

Huge round oranges of light
Ripen against the thin dark of the city sky,
Spilling their juice in warm pools
   on bare dry pavements.
Below them blink the traffic lights
   like the eyes of enormous cats
Crouching in the dark –
Crouching and breathing with the heavy purr of traffic;
And winking tail lights slide and dart
   like goldfish
In the pale streams pouring from
   shop windows.

Margaret Greaves

A HAIKU YEARBOOK

Snow in January
Looking for ledges
To hide in unmelted.

February evening:
A cold puddle of petrol
Makes its own rainbow.

Wind in March:
No leaves left
For its stiff summons.

April sunlight:
Even the livid bricks
Muted a little.

Wasp in May
Storing his venom
For a long summer.

Morning in June:
On the sea's horizon
A white island, alone.

July evening:
Sour reek of beer
Warm by the river.

August morning:
A squirrel leaps and
Only one branch moves.

September chestnuts:
Falling too early,
Split white before birth.

October garden:
At the top of the tree
A thrush stabs an apple.

November morning:
A whiff of cordite
Caught in the leaf mould

Sun in December:
In his box of straw
The tortoise wakes.

Anthony Thwaite

IMAGINE

Imagine a snail
As big as a whale,
Imagine a lark
As big as a shark,
Imagine a bee
As big as a tree.
Imagine a toad
As long as a road,
Imagine a hare
As big as a chair,
Imagine a goat
As long as a boat
And a flea the same size as me.

Roland Egan

NOVEMBER STORY

The evening had caught cold;
Its eyes were blurred.
It had a dripping nose
And its tongue was furred.

I sat in a warm bar
After the day's work;
November snuffled outside,
Greasing the sidewalk.

But soon I had to go
Out into the night
Where shadows prowled the alleys,
Hiding from the light.

But light shone at the corner
On the pavement where
A man had fallen over
Or been knocked down there.

His legs on the slimed concrete
Were splayed out wide;
He had been propped against a lamp-post;
His head lolled to one side.

A victim of crime or accident,
An image of fear,
He remained quite motionless
As I drew near.

Then a thin voice startled silence
From a doorway close by
Where an urchin hid from the wind:
'Spare a penny for the guy!'

I gave the boy some money
And hastened on.
A voice called, 'Thank you guv'nor!'
And the words upon

The wincing air seemed strange –
So hoarse and deep –
As if the guy had spoken
In his restless sleep.

Vernon Scannell

WATER PICTURE

In the pond in the park
all things are double:
Long buildings hang and
wriggle gently. Chimneys
are bent legs bouncing
on clouds below. A flag
wags like a fishhook
down there in the sky.

The arched stone bridge
is an eye, with underlid
in the water. In its lens
dip crinkled heads with hats
that don't fall off. Dogs go by,
barking on their backs.
A baby, taken to feed the
ducks, dangles upside-down,
a pink balloon for a buoy.

Treetops deploy a haze of
cherry bloom for roots,
where birds coast belly-up
in the glass bowl of a hill;
from its bottom a bunch
of peanut-munching children
is suspended by their
sneakers, waveringly.

A swan, with twin necks
forming the figure three,
steers between two dimpled
towers doubled. Fondly
hissing, she kisses herself,
and all the scene is troubled:
water-windows splinter,
tree-limbs tangle, the bridge
folds like a fan.

May Swenson

A HOT DAY

Cottonwool clouds loiter.
A lawnmower, very far,
Birrs. Then a bee comes
To a crimson rose and softly,
Deftly and fatly crams
A velvet body in.

A tree, June-lazy, makes
A tent of dim green light.
Sunlight weaves in the leaves,
Honey-light laced with leaf-light,
Green interleaved with gold.

Sunlight gathers its rays
In sheaves, which the wind unweaves
And then reweaves – the wind
That puffs a smell of grass
Through the heat-heavy, trembling
Summer pool of air.

A. S. J. Tessimond

SEA'S CAPE

I
see
gulls
Icy
gulls
I see
gulls screaming
– Aye –
I see seagulls
screaming, see
Ai YUY –
scream
. . . 'Ice CREAM'
the seagulls
seem to scream
Hi Hi *eee*
Ye – Icy seagulls!

I see
Gulls   see
eyes

cream

Michael Horovitz

TYPEWRITING CLASS

Dear Miss Hinson
I am spitting
In front of my top ratter
With the rest of my commercesnail sturdy students
Triping you this later.
The truce is Miss Hinson
I am not hippy with my cross.
Every day on Woundsday
I sit in my dusk
with my type rutter
Trooping without lurking at the lattice
All sorts of weird messengers.
To give one exam pill,
'The quick down socks. . . .
The quick brine pox. . . .
The sick frown box. . . .
The sick down jocks
Humps over the hazy bog'
When everyone kows
That a sick down jock
Would not be seen dead near a hazy bog.
Another one we tripe is;
'Now is the tame
For all guide men
To cram to the head
Of the pratty.'
To may why of sinking
I that is all you get to tripe
In true whelks of stirdy
Then I am thinking of changing
To crookery classes.
I would sooner end up a crook
Than a shirt hand trappist
Any die of the wink.
I have taken the tremble, Miss Hinson
To trip you this later
So that you will be able
To understand my indignation.
I must clothe now
As the Bill is groaning
                              Yours fitfully. . . . .

Gareth Owen

74

THE MEADOW MOUSE

I

In a shoe-box stuffed in an old nylon stocking
Sleeps the baby mouse I found in the meadow,
Where he trembled and shook beneath a stick
Till I caught him up by the tail and brought him in,
Cradled in my hand,
A little quaker, the whole body of him trembling,
His absurd whiskers sticking out like a cartoon-mouse,
His feet like small leaves,
Little lizard-feet,
Whitish and spread wide when he tried to struggle away,
Wriggling like a minuscule puppy.
Now he's eaten his three kinds of cheese and drunk from
    his bottle-cap watering trough –

So much he just lies in one corner,
His tail curled under him, his belly big
As his head; his bat-like ears
Twitching, tilting towards the least sound.

Do I imagine he no longer trembles
When I come close to him?
He seems no longer to tremble.

II

But this morning the shoe-box house on the back porch is empty.
Where has he gone, my meadow mouse,
My thumb of a child that nuzzled in my palm? –
To run under the hawk's wing,
Under the eye of the great owl watching from the elm-tree,
To live by courtesy of the shrike, the snake, the tom-cat.

I think of the nestling fallen into the deep grass,
The turtle gasping in the dusty rubble of the highway,
The paralytic stunned in the tub, and the water rising –
All things innocent, hapless, forsaken.

Theodore Roethke

DEATH OF A BIRD

After those first days
When we had placed him in his iron cage
And made a space for him
From such

Outrageous cage of wire,
Long and shallow, where the sunlight fell
Through the air, onto him;
After

He had been fed for three days
Suddenly, in that sunlight before noon
He was dead with no
Pretence.

He did not say goodbye,
He did not say thankyou, but he died then
Lying flat on the rigid
Wires

Of his cage, his gold
Beak shut tight, which once in hunger had
Opened as a trap
And then

Swiftly closed again,
Swallowing quickly what I had given him;
How can I say I am sorry
He died.

Seeing him lie there dead,
Death's friend with death, I was angry he
Had gone without pretext or warning
With no

Suggestion first he should go,
Since I had fed him, then put wires round him,
Bade him hop across
The bars of my hands.

I asked him only that
He should desire his life. He had become
Of us a black friend with
A gold mouth

Shrilly singing through
The heat. The labour of the black bird! I
Cannot understand why
He is dead.

I bury him familiarly.
His heritage is a small brown garden.
Something is added to the everlasting earth;
From my mind a space is taken away.

Jon Silkin

MUSICAL CHAIRS

Father, weighty as a minim —
Ample the armchair that has him in.

Grandma, like a semibreve,
Rests on the couch she cannot leave.

Mother, an anxious dotted crotchet
Out of the game, prefers to watch it.

Grandpa, a somewhat tiresome quaver,
Is hardly on his best behaviour.

Round him the children, demi-semis,
Fidget and tumble as they please.

The cat meanwhile lies fast asleep,
Oblivious of the times they keep.

John Mole

THE FLY

How large unto the tiny fly
Must little things appear!
— A rosebud like a feather bed,
Its prickle like a spear,
A dewdrop like a looking-glass
A hair like golden wire;
The smallest grain of mustard-seed
As fierce as coals of fire;
A loaf of bread, a lofty hill;
A wasp, a cruel leopard;
And specks of salt as bright to see
As lambkins to a shepherd.

Walter de la Mare

A CASE OF MURDER

They should not have left him there alone,
Alone that is except for the cat.
He was only nine, not old enough
To be left alone in a basement flat,
Alone, that is, except for the cat.
A dog would have been a different thing,
A big gruff dog with slashing jaws,
But a cat with round eyes mad as gold,
Plump as a cushion with tucked-in paws —
Better have left him with a fair-sized rat!
But what they did was leave him with a cat.
He hated that cat; he watched it sit,
A buzzing machine of soft black stuff,
He sat and watched and he hated it,
Snug in its fur, hot blood in a muff,
And its mad gold stare and the way it sat
Crooning dark warmth: he loathed all that.
So he took Daddy's stick and he hit the cat.
Then quick as a sudden crack in glass
It hissed, black flash, to a hiding place
In the dust and dark beneath the couch,
And he followed the grin on his new-made face,
A wide-eyed, frightened snarl of a grin,
And he took the stick and he thrust it in,
Hard and quick in the furry dark.
The black fur squealed and he felt his skin
Prickle with sparks of dry delight.
Then the cat again came into sight,
Shot for the door that wasn't quite shut,
But the boy, quick too, slammed fast the door:
The cat, half-through, was cracked like a nut
And the soft black thud was dumped on the floor.
Then the boy was suddenly terrified
And he bit his knuckles and cried and cried;
But he had to do something with the dead thing there.
His eyes squeezed beads of salty prayer
But the wound of fear gaped wide and raw;
He dared not touch the thing with his hands
So he fetched a spade and shovelled it
And dumped the load of heavy fur
In the spidery cupboard under the stair
Where it's been for years, and though it died
It's grown in that cupboard and its hot low purr

Grows slowly louder year by year:
There'll not be a corner for the boy to hide
When the cupboard swells and all sides split
And the huge black cat pads out of it.

Vernon Scannell

Here are the original versions of the two 'jumbled rhymes' on pages 20 and 21.

THE TIRED CATERPILLAR

A tired old caterpillar went to sleep
In a hole in the forest, snug and deep.
And he said, as he softly curled in his nest . . .
'Crawling is pleasant but rest is best.'
He slept through the Winter long and cold,
All tightly up in his blanket rolled,
But at last he woke on a warm Spring day
To find that Winter had gone away.
He felt and fluttered his golden wings:
No need to crawl over sticks and things.
'Oh, earth is good for a butterfly,
But the sky is best when we learn to fly!'

Clive Sansom

ELEPHANTS WALKING

We're swaying through the jungle
Dizzy with the heat
Searching for a water-hole
To cool our heavy feet.
Trample on the grasses;
Then stop and breathe the scent
Of flower and leaf – and tiger!
And watch the way he went.
Then on again we stumble,
Searching for a drink;
We find a spilling river,
And into it we sink.

Ruth Sansom

Book List

If you would like to read more poems by any of the writers named in this book, then here is a list of authors and titles for you to explore. But remember, no list of writers is ever complete. There are many other books of poems on the shelf, just waiting to be discovered — by you!

Cock-a-doodle Don't, Ivor Cutler, Dobson
Meal One, Ivor Cutler, Armada
Animal House, Ivor Cutler, Heinemann
Your Turn Next, Margaret Greaves, Methuen
Growing Up: Selected Poems and Pictures 1951 – 1979 Michael Horovitz, Allison and Busby
Meet My Folks!; *Season Songs*; *Flowers and Insects: Poems*, Ted Hughes, Faber and Faber
Under the North Star, Ted Hughes, Faber and Faber
Moon-bells and other Poems, Ted Hughes, Chatto and Windus
Sky in the Pie, Roger McGough, Puffin
Nailing the Shadow, Roger McGough, Viking Kestrel
Nothingmas Day Adrian Mitchell, (Illustrated by John Lawrence) Allison and Busby
Once there were Dragons, John Mole, Andre Deutsch
Boo to a Goose, John Mole, Peterloo Poets
In and Out of the Apple, and *Feeding the Lake*, John Mole, Secker and Warburg
From Glasgow to Saturn, and *Selected Poems*, Edwin Morgan, Carcanet
Song of the City and *Salford Road*, Gareth Owen, Fontana Young Lions
Hero Dust, Tom Pickard, Allison and Busby
Peacock Pie, Walter De La Mare, Faber and Faber
Collected Poems, Theodore Roethke, Faber and Faber
Wouldn't You Like to Know Michael Rosen, Puffin
The H.Y.P.N.O.T.I.S.E.R, Michael Rosen, Andre Deutsch
Complete Poems, Carl Sandburg, Jonathan Cape
Mastering the Craft, Vernon Scannell, Pergamon
New and Collected Poems, and *Winterlude*, Vernon Scannell, Robson Books
Poems New and Selected, Jon Silkin, Chatto and Windus
To Mix With Time, May Swenson, Charles Scribner
Selection, A. J. Tessimond, Faber and Faber
Poems 1953–1983 Anthony Thwaite, Secker and Warburg
Rabbiting On, Kit Wright, Fontana Lions